Quick & Easy
Sensational
DESSERTS

Judi Olstein

JG
PRESS

Published by
World Publications, Inc.
455 Somerset Avenue
North Dighton, MA 02764

Produced by The Triangle Group, Ltd.
227 Park Avenue
Hoboken, NJ 07030

Editorial: Jake Elwell
Design: Tony Meisel
Printing: Cronion S.A., Barcelona

ISBN 1-57215-001-7

Printed in Spain

Contents

3

4

Introduction

America has a big sweet tooth! All the cakes, cookies, ice cream, pies, candies, chocolates and other sweetmeats make us one of the biggest consumers of sugar in the world. Luckily we have good dentists.

However, in moderation, desserts—not all-day sweet munchies—bring a meal to a satisfying conclusion. Or they can be eaten in the afternoon with tea or coffee. The key is to eat only one portion of sweet dessert per day, not one after lunch, one after dinner and one as a snack before retiring.

In this book you will not find the spun sugar fantasies and elaborate decorative filigree of a professional baker. These desserts are to be made with relative ease at home. Some are, of course, more complicated than others, but all are within the reach of the average cook and home baker.

If you're sure of yourself, you can elaborate on these recipes, but all have been tested and measurements and baking temperatures are not something to fool around with. Baking is the application of practical chemistry and should be treated with the precision and respect it demands.

A word of advice. Use the best ingredients—fresh flour, fresh eggs, the best sweet butter you can buy and genuine, natural flavorings and essences. Stale, old ingredients will show up in the finished product, and artificial flavorings will impart an indescribably metallic, oversweet taste to everything they enter into. Care taken up front will reap rich rewards later on—when you garner the praise.

After you have made the original recipe a few times, you can substitute, add icing or decorations. But none of these desserts need further elaboration. All are deeply satisfying and will bring smiles of pleasure to friends and family alike.

6 | Plain Pastry

2 cups flour
1/2 teaspoon salt
3/4 cup butter of vegetable shortening; chilled
4 tablespoons cold water

Sift the flour with the salt into a large mixing bowl. Cut in the shortening with a pastry blender, two knives or your fingertips until the mixture is crumbly.

Sprinkle cold water over the flour mixture. Mix lightly with a fork until the dough holds together. Press lightly into a ball. Wrap in plastic and chill in the refrigerator for at least 1 hour.

Sour Cream-Apple Pie

6 to 8 tart apples, peeled, cored and thinly sliced
1/2 cup sour cream
1/4 cup sugar
3/4 cup gingersnap crumbs
1 tablespoon flour
1/2 teaspoon cinnamon
1/4 teaspoon nutmeg
1/4 teaspoon salt
1/2 cup melted butter
1/2 cup pure maple syrup
1 pastry for a 9-inch pie

Preheat the oven to 350 degrees F.

Place the pastry into a 9-inch pie pan. Crimp around the edges.

In a bowl combine the apples and sour cream. Place half the sliced apples in the pastry shell.

In a mixing bowl combine the sugar, gingersnap crumbs, flour, cinnamon, salt, nutmeg, and butter. Mix until well blended.

Sprinkle half this mixture over the apples in the pie shell. Place the remaining apple slices in a layer over the crumbs. Sprinkle with remaining crumbs.

Bake 45 minutes. Heat the maple syrup to the boiling point and pour evenly over the pie. Bake 15 to minutes 20 longer or until the apples are tender. Serves 6.

Pumpkin Pie

1 cup puréed pumpkin, canned or fresh
3 eggs separated
1 cup sugar
3/4 cup milk
2 tablespoons melted butter
1/2 teaspoons salt
1/2 teaspoons ground ginger
1/4 teaspoons grated nutmeg
1 teaspoon cinnamon
1 tablespoon unflavored gelatin
1/4 cup cold water
1 pastry for 9-inch pie

Preheat the oven to 450 degrees F.

Place the pastry into a 9-inch pie pan. Crimp around the edges. Prick with a fork and line with aluminum foil and weight with beans, rice or pie weights. Bake for 7 minutes; remove the weights and foil and continue baking until golden brown. Remove from the oven and let cool.

Place the pumpkin in the top of a double boiler, over hot but not boiling water. Beat the egg yolks and add to the pumpkin. Add 1/2 cup of the sugar, milk, butter, salt, ginger, nutmeg and cinnamon. Cook, stirring constantly, until mixture thickens and reaches the consistency of custard. Remove from the heat.

Soften the gelatin in the cold water. Combine the gelatin with the pumpkin mixture and stir until dissolved. Chill until slightly thickened.

In a small bowl, beat the egg whites until they are stiff but not dry. Gradually beat in the remaining 1/2 cup sugar. Fold into the pumpkin mixture. Pour the mixture into pastry shell. Chill for 3 hours or until firm. If desired serve with whipped cream. Serves 8.

8

Pumpkin Pie

9

Blueberry Pie

10 Blueberry Pie

1 quart fresh blueberries
1 cup sugar
1 tablespoon flour
1/4 teaspoon grated nutmeg
2 tablespoons butter
 pastry for 2-crust 9-inch pie

Preheat the oven to 350 degrees F.
   Wash the blueberries and drain well.
   Line a 9-inch pie pan with one of the pie crusts, trimming so
that about 1/2 inch hangs over the edge. Reserve the second crust
for the top of the pie.
   Mix 1 tablespoon sugar with the flour and sprinkle into the pie
crust. Fill the crust with blueberries and sprinkle with nutmeg.
Sprinkle with the remaining sugar and dot evenly with the butter.
   Place the second crust over the top to cover. Tuck the top crust
under the overlap of the bottom crust and seal by crimping the
edges firmly together. Prick the top of the pie to let the steam
escape.
   Place the pie on the lowest shelf of the oven for 10 minutes.
Then move it to the middle shelf and lower the heat to
300 degrees F. Continue baking for about 30 minutes or until
crust is golden. Serves 8.

Rice Pudding

2 cups medium or long-grain cooked rice
1 cup milk
1/3 cup light cream
1/8 teaspoon salt
1/3 cup sugar
1 tablespoon butter, softened
1 teaspoon vanilla
3 eggs
1 teaspoon grated lemon rind
1/2 cup currants or raisins
1/2 cup slivered almonds, crushed

Preheat the oven to 325 degrees F.

Place the cooked rice in a large mixing bowl. Add to the rice the milk, cream, salt, sugar, butter, vanilla, eggs, lemon and currants. Mix well. Place the mixture in a well-greased baking pan or casserole. Sprinkle with the almonds.

Bake in the oven for 50 minutes or until set. Serve hot or cold. Serves 6.

Pound Cake

1 pound sweet butter
1 pound sugar
10 eggs, separated
4 cups flour
1/2 teaspoon salt
1 teaspoon baking powder
1 teaspoon vanilla
2 tablespoons freshly grated lemon rind

Butter 2 12-inch loaf pans and dust lightly with flour. Set aside.

In a large bowl cream the butter. Gradually add the sugar and continue creaming until the mixture is light and fluffy.

In a separate bowl beat the egg yolks. Add the yolks to the butter mixture, beating constantly.

In another bowl, or a large sheet of wax paper, sift together the flour, salt, and baking powder 4 times.

Gradually add the flour to the butter mixture. Mix thoroughly. Add the vanilla and lemon rind. Mix well.

Preheat the oven to 300 degrees F.

In a small bowl beat the egg whites until they are stiff but not dry. Fold into the batter.

Pour half the mixture into each of the loaf pans. Bake for 1 to 1 1/2 hours or until a cake tester inserted into the middle of the loaf comes out clean. Each loaf serves 8 to 10.

12

13

14 | Lemon Meringue Pie

1 cup sugar
2 tablespoons cornstarch
1/4 teaspoon salt
1 1/2 cups hot water
1 1/2 cups bread crumbs
3 eggs, separated
1 tablespoon butter
freshly grated peel of 1 large lemon
juice of 2 medium lemons
1 pastry for 9-inch pie shell
6 tablespoons water
1/4 teaspoon salt

Preheat the oven to 400 degrees F.

Fit the crust into a 9-inch pie pan and flute the edges. Prick the pastry all over with a fork and line with aluminum foil and beans, rice or pie weights. Bake for 10 minutes. Remove the pan from the oven and take off the aluminum foil and weights. Return to the oven and bake an additional 10 minutes or until golden. Remove from the oven and cool.

Beat the egg yolks in a bowl.

In the top of a double boiler, over hot not boiling water, mix the sugar, cornstarch and salt. Add the hot water and stir, then beat until the mixture is smooth. Add the bread crumbs. Cook over the water, stirring constantly, until the mixture is thick and smooth.

Stir 2 tablespoons of the bread crumb mixture into the beaten eggs. Add the egg yolk mixture back to the crumb mixture in the double boiler. Cook for 2 to 3 minutes. Remove from the heat and add the butter, lemon rind, and lemon juice. Cool slightly.

In a small bowl beat the egg whites, with the salt until foamy. Gradually beat in 6 tablespoons of sugar. Beat until whites are stiff but not dry.

Pour the cooled filling into the baked pie shell. Pile the egg whites lightly on top of the filling. Cover the filling and the edges of the pie completely.

Bake for 5 minutes or until lightly browned. Remove from the oven and cool. Serves 8.

Blueberry Butter Cake

1 cup sweet butter, softened
2 1/2 cups flour
1 1/4 cups sugar
4 eggs
2 1/2 teaspoons baking powder
1/4 teaspoon salt
1 1/2 teaspoons vanilla extract
1 1/2 cups fresh blueberries, rinsed and drained
1 cup chilled heavy cream

Preheat the oven to 375 degrees F. Generously butter and flour an 8-inch spring form cake pan. Set aside.

In a large mixing bowl cream the butter and sugar together until light and fluffy. Add the eggs one at a time, beating well after each addition.

In a bowl combine 2 1/4 cups flour with the baking powder and salt. Gradually, beat the flour mixture into the butter-egg mixture. Add the vanilla extract and beat to combine.

Place the blueberries in a small bowl and toss with the remaining 1/4 cup flour. Coat the berries evenly. Gently fold the berries into the batter.

Turn the batter into the prepared pan. Bake for 1 hour or until a cake tester inserted into the center comes out clean.

Remove from the oven. Remove the sides of the pan. Cool cake for 20 minutes.

Beat the chilled cream in a chilled mixing bowl. Sweeten with a little sugar if desired. Beat the cream until it is thick enough to form peaks. Serve the cream with the warm cake.

Blueberry Butter Cake

Chocolate Bundt Cake

18 | Chocolate Bundt Cake

3 cups sifted cake flour
1 cup Dutch-process unsweetened cocoa
1 tablespoon baking powder
1 teaspoon salt
2 3/4 cups sugar
1 cup sweet butter, softened
1 1/2 cups milk
1 tablespoon vanilla extract
3 large eggs
1/4 cup light cream
1 cup coarsely chopped walnuts
1 1/4 cups semisweet chocolate pieces
1/2 cup dark raisins
1/2 cup golden raisins

Preheat the oven to 325 degrees F. Generously butter and flour a 12-cup bundt pan (or round springform). Set aside.

Into a large bowl sift together the flour, cocoa, baking powder and salt. Add the sugar and stir to combine. Make a well in the center of the dry ingredients and add the butter. Mix until well combined.

Using an electric mixer, gradually beat in the milk, and the vanilla extract. Beat for 7 minutes. Scrape down the sides with a rubber spatula when necessary.

Add the eggs, one at a time, beating well after each addition. Add the cream and beat well to blend.

Add the walnuts, chocolate pieces, raisins, and golden raisins. Stir until thoroughly incorporated into the batter.

Turn the batter into the prepared pan and bake in the oven for 1 hour and 40 minutes or until a cake tester inserted into the center of the cake comes out clean.

Remove from the oven and cool in the pan on a wire rack for 10 minutes. Turn cake out onto rack and cool completely.
Serves 10-12.

Chocolate Fudge Cake

4 ounces unsweetened chocolate
1/2 cup hot water
1/2 cup sugar
2 cups flour
1 teaspoon baking soda
1 teaspoon salt
1/2 cup sweet butter
1 1/4 cups sugar
3 eggs
1 teaspoon vanilla extract
2/3 cup milk

FROSTING
4 ounces unsweetened chocolate
1 1/2 cups milk
4 cups sugar
1/8 teaspoon salt
4 teaspoons light corn syrup
1/4 cup sweet butter
2 teaspoons vanilla extract

Preheat the oven to 350 degrees F. Butter and flour two 9-inch square pans. Set aside. Combine the chocolate and water in the top of a double boiler. Cook over hot, not boiling water until the chocolate is melted. Add 1/2 cup sugar and cook for 2 minutes longer. Set aside.

Onto a large piece of wax paper sift the flour, baking soda and salt. Sift together twice more and set aside.

Cream the butter in a mixing bowl. Add 1 1/4 cups sugar. Cream together until light and fluffy. Add the eggs, one at a time, beating well after each addition. Add the vanilla. Add the flour alternately with the milk, beating well after each addition. Begin and end with the flour. Add the chocolate mixture and blend well.

Pour the batter into the prepared pans. Bake for 25 to 30 minutes or until a cake tester inserted into the center comes out clean. Cool pans on racks for 10 minutes. Turn out and continue to cool.

Frost when cool, as follows: Place the chocolate and milk in a heavy saucepan. Cook over a low heat, stirring constantly, until well blended.

Add the sugar, salt and corn syrup. Stir until the sugar is dissolved. Boil the mixture over very low heat, stirring occasionally, until small amounts dropped into cold water form soft balls. This will be when the mixture is approximately 234 to 240 degrees F. on a candy thermometer.

Remove the saucepan from the heat. Add the butter and vanilla and mix well. Cool to lukewarm and then beat until creamy. Serves 8.

Chocolate Fudge Cake

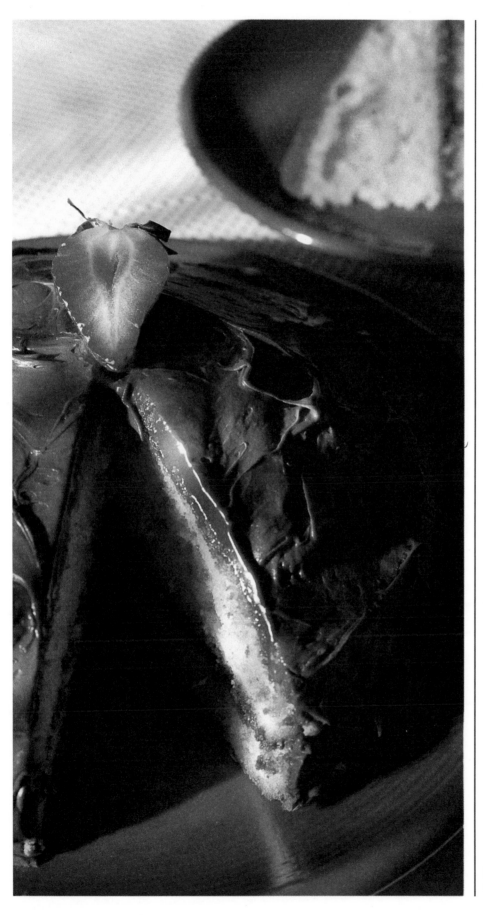

21

Chocolate-Frosted
Yellow Cake

22 | Chocolate-Frosted Yellow Cake

1 3/4 cups sifted cake flour
1/2 teaspoon salt
2 teaspoons baking powder
1/2 cup softened butter
1 cup sugar
2 eggs, lightly beaten
1/2 cup milk
1/2 teaspoon pure vanilla extract

FROSTING

1 cup sugar
4 tablespoons cake flour
4 ounces unsweetened chocolate, cut into pieces
1 1/2 cups milk
2 tablespoons sweet butter

Preheat the oven to 375 degrees F. Generously butter and flour two 9-inch round cake pans.

Into a bowl sift together the cake flour, salt and baking powder. Set aside.

In a large bowl cream the butter until soft and light. Add the sugar, a little at a time, and mix until very fluffy. Add the eggs and mix until well blended.

Add the flour alternately with the milk to the butter mixture. Beat well but only until just mixed. Add the vanilla and mix to blend.

Transfer the batter to the prepared pans; divide evenly. Bake for 25-30 minutes or until a cake tester inserted into the center comes out clean. Remove from the oven and turn out onto a wire rack. Invert so that layers are right-side up and cool completely. Make the frosting while the layers cool. Frost as follows:

In a medium-sized saucepan combine the sugar, cake flour and chocolate. Add the milk and mix well.

Cook over moderate heat, stirring constantly, until the mixture boils and is thick and smooth. Remove from the heat. Add the butter and stir to blend. Cool before using. Serves 8.

Strawberry Shortcake

1 3/4 cups sifted cake flour
1/2 teaspoon salt
2 teaspoons baking powder
1/2 cup softened butter
1 cup sugar
2 eggs, lightly beaten
1/2 cup milk
1/2 teaspoon pure vanilla extract

TOPPING
4 cups fresh strawberries
1/3 cup sugar
1 cup heavy cream
1/2 cup confectioner's sugar

Preheat the oven to 375 degrees F. Generously butter and flour two 9-inch round cake pans.

Into a bowl sift together the cake flour, salt and baking powder. Set aside.

In a large bowl cream the butter until soft and light. Add the sugar, a little at a time, and mix until very fluffy. Add the eggs and mix until well blended.

Add the flour alternately with the milk to the butter mixture. Beat well but only until just mixed. Add the vanilla and mix to blend.

Transfer the batter to the prepared pans; divide evenly. Bake for 25-30 minutes or until a cake tester inserted into the center comes out clean. Remove from the oven and turn out onto a wire rack. Invert so that layers are right-side up and cool completely.

Clean, hull and quarter the berries. If they are very large, slice them. Combine the berries with the sugar. Adjust the sugar to taste. Allow to stand for 15 minutes.

In a bowl beat the cream with the confectioner's sugar until it is a spreading consistency. Chill briefly.

Transfer one cake layer to a serving plate and frost with the cream. Top with some of the strawberries and then place the remaining layer on top. Finish frosting the cake with the cream and spoon strawberries on top and around the cake. You may wish to drain some of the liquid before using. Refrigerate before serving. Serves 8.

Strawberry Shortcake

Chocolate Chip
Cheesecake

26 | Chocolate Chip Cheesecake

1 1/4 cups chocolate cookie crumbs
1/4 cup sweet butter, melted
1 tablespoon sugar
2 1/2 pounds cream cheese, softened
1 3/4 cups sugar
1/4 cup flour
1 teaspoon vanilla extract
5 large eggs
2 egg yolks
1/4 cup heavy cream
1/2 cup very small semisweet chocolate pieces

In a bowl combine the cookie crumbs, butter and one tablespoon sugar. Mix well. Press mixture into the bottom of a buttered 9-inch spring form pan. Refrigerate until needed.

Preheat the oven to 475 degrees F.

In a large bowl beat together the cream cheese and sugar until light and fluffy. Add the whole eggs and egg yolks, one at a time, beating well after each addition. Add the flour and vanilla extract and continue beating until the mixture is smooth. Scrape down the sides of the bowl with a rubber spatula. Stir in the chocolate pieces.

Turn the batter into the prepared pan. Place pan on a baking sheet. Bake for 10 minutes. Lower the temperature to 250 degrees F. and bake for 1 hour. Turn off the oven; let the cake cool in the oven for 1 hour. Open the oven door part way and let cake cool for 30 minutes longer. Remove from the oven and cool on a wire rack to room temperature.

Refrigerate at least 8 hours or overnight before serving.
Serves 10.

Lemon-Orange Cheesecake

4 cups graham cracker crumbs
1 cup sweet butter, melted
2 tablespoons unflavored gelatin
3/4 cup sugar
5 large eggs, separated
dash of salt
1/3 cup milk, scalded
24 ounces cream cheese, softened
1/3 cup lemon juice
1/4 cup orange-flavored liqueur
1/2 teaspoon vanilla extract
1/2 cup sugar
finely grated rind of 2 lemons

Preheat oven to 350 degrees F.

In a large bowl combine the graham cracker crumbs and melted butter. Mix well. Remove 1/3 cup of the crumbs and set aside. Press the remaining crumbs into the bottom and up the sides of a buttered 10-inch spring form pan. Bake crust for 12 to 15 minutes or until firm. Remove from the oven and cool on a wire rack. Turn off the oven.

In a small cup, soften the gelatin in the cold water for 4 to 5 minutes

In the top part of a double boiler, combine the 3/4 cup sugar, egg yolks, and salt. Beat well. Place over slowly simmering water. Add the scalded milk, a little at a time, beating constantly until thick and smooth, approximately 5 minutes. Add the gelatin mixture and stir until totally dissolved. Remove from the heat and cool.

In a large bowl beat the cream cheese until smooth. Add a small amount of the egg yolk mixture and beat well. Fold in the remaining egg yolks. Add the lemon juice, orange liqueur and vanilla extract. Fold in until well blended.

In a large bowl beat the egg whites until soft peaks begin to form. Add the 1/2 cup sugar, a little at a time, beating until stiff but not dry. Gently fold egg whites into cheese mixture.

Turn the mixture into prepared pan. Smooth the top with a rubber spatula and sprinkle with the reserved crumbs and the grated lemon rind. Refrigerate for 8 hours or overnight. Serves 10.

Lemon-Orange
Cheesecake

Oatmeal Cookies

30 | Oatmeal Cookies

1 cup flour
1 cup sweet butter, softened
3/4 cup firmly packed light brown sugar
1/2 cup sugar
1 large egg
3 tablespoons water
3/4 teaspoon salt
1/2 teaspoon baking soda
3/4 teaspoon vanilla extract
3 1/2 cups quick-cooking rolled oats (not instant)
1 cup raisins (optional)

Preheat the oven to 375 degrees F. Heavily butter two baking sheets. Set aside.

In a large bowl combine the flour, butter, brown sugar, sugar, egg, water, salt, baking soda and vanilla extract. Beat the mixture with an electric mixer at a low speed until well blended. Scrape the bowl with a rubber spatula when necessary. Add the oats to the mixture. Using a spoon, stir until thoroughly combined. If you wish, add the raisins and stir.

Drop the dough by heaping tablespoons onto the baking sheets. Space cookies about 2-inches apart.

Bake for 10-12 minutes or until golden. Remove from the oven and carefully transfer cookies to a wire rack. Cool on wire racks. Store in airtight containers. Makes 30 cookies.

Chocolate Chip Cookies

1/2 cup sweet butter, softened
1/2 cup sugar
1/4 cup firmly packed light brown sugar
1 egg, beaten
1 teaspoon vanilla extract
1 cup flour
1/2 teaspoon baking soda
1/2 cup chopped walnuts, pecans or hazelnuts
6 ounces semisweet chocolate pieces

Preheat the oven to 375 degrees F. Lightly butter two baking sheets. Set aside.

In a large bowl cream the butter until soft. Gradually beat in the sugar and brown sugar. Beat in the eggs and vanilla extract.

Add the flour and baking soda to the mixture. Stir until smooth. Stir in the nuts and chocolate bits, making sure they are evenly distributed throughout the batter.

Drop scant teaspoons 2 inches apart onto the baking sheets. Bake for 8 to 10 minutes or until edges are beginning to brown. Transfer to racks and cool. Makes 48 cookies.

Ginger-Molasses Cookies

6 1/2 cups flour
1 tablespoon baking soda
1 tablespoon ground cinnamon
2 1/4 teaspoon ground ginger
1 teaspoon nutmeg
2 cups sweet butter, softened
3/4 cup packed light brown sugar
3/4 cup molasses
1/4 cup water
1 1/2 teaspoons salt
3 large eggs, at room temperature
1/2 cup white sugar

Into a large bowl sift together the flour, baking soda, cinnamon, ginger and nutmeg. Set aside.

In another large bowl, beat the butter until soft and smooth. Add the brown sugar and molasses, water and salt. Beat together until the mixture is light and fluffy. Add the eggs, one at a time, beating well after each addition. Scrape the sides of the bowl with a rubber spatula as needed. Gradually add the flour mixture and beat until well mixed. Cover bowl and refrigerate dough for at least 20 hours.

Preheat the oven to 350 degrees F. Remove the dough from the refrigerator. Shape dough into 2-inch balls and roll each in the white sugar. Space cookies 3 inches apart on ungreased baking sheets. Bake for 15 to 18 minutes or until cookies are lightly browned and set. Remove cookies from the oven and transfer to wire racks to cool. Makes 30 cookies.

Ginger-Molasses
Cookies

Nut Brownies

34 Nut Brownies

4 ounces unsweetened chocolate
1 cup butter, cut into pieces
1 3/4 cups sugar
4 eggs
1 1/2 cups flour
1/4 teaspoon salt
1 1/2 teaspoons vanilla extract
1 1/2 cups coarsely chopped pecans or walnuts

Preheat the oven to 375 degrees F. Butter and flour a 9 x 9 x 2-inch square baking pan. Set aside.

In the top of a double boiler, over hot but not boiling water, melt the chocolate. Add the butter gradually, stir well after each addition. Add the sugar and stir until completely dissolved. Remove from the heat.

Add the eggs one at a time, beat after each addition. Beat in the flour, salt and vanilla extract. Add the nuts and stir.

Turn the batter into the prepared pan. Bake for 40 minutes or until brownies begin to shrink away from the sides of the pan. Do not overbake. Cool in pan, then cut into squares. Makes 16 to 20 brownies.

Pecan Meringues

1 egg white
1 cup sifted light brown sugar
1 1/2 cups pecan halves
1/4 cup pine nuts

Preheat the oven to 250 degrees F. Heavily grease two baking sheets. Set aside.

In a mixing bowl beat the egg white until it is stiff enough to form a soft peak. Beat in the brown sugar, a little at a time, until the mixture is stiff and no longer glossy. Gently fold in the pecan halves. Drop the batter by well-rounded tablespoons onto the baking sheets. Use a second spoon to help slide the batter off the tablespoon and onto the sheet. Space the cookies 1 inch apart. Decorate each meringue with pine nuts.

Bake for 30 minutes or until the cookies are pale brown.

Remove sheets from the oven. With a wide metal spatula transfer the cookies to cooling racks. Store airtight. Makes 24 cookies.

Shortbread

4 cups flour
2 cups sweet butter, softened
1 1/2 cups confectioners' sugar
1 teaspoon baking powder
1/4 teaspoon salt

Preheat the oven to 325 degrees F. In a large bowl combine the flour, butter, confectioners' sugar, baking powder and salt. Using your hands, mix the ingredients until well blended. The dough will be soft.

Evenly distribute the dough between two 9-inch round pans. Pat down gently. Prick the top of the dough with a fork all over.

Bake for 45 minutes or until golden. Remove from the oven. While the shortbread is warm cut it with a sharp knife in 12 equal wedges. Cool in pans on racks. Makes 24 wedges.

38 | Sugar Cookies

2 cups flour
1/2 teaspoon baking powder
1/2 teaspoon baking soda
1/4 teaspoon salt
1/2 cup vegetable oil or 1/2 cup solid vegetable shortening
1/2 cup sugar
1 egg
1 teaspoon vanilla extract
3 tablespoons milk
sugar for sprinkling

Preheat the oven to 375 degrees F. Lightly butter two baking sheets and set aside. In a medium size bowl sift together the flour, baking powder, baking soda and salt.

In a large bowl, beat the oil or shortening and sugar together. Beat in the egg and the vanilla extract. Add the flour mixture and the milk, alternately, beginning and ending with the flour. If dough is sticky refrigerate briefly.

Lightly flour a working surface and roll the dough out to approximately 1/8-inch thickness. Using a 3-inch round biscuit cutter, cut out the cookies. Transfer to the baking sheets. Continue to cut the cookies and reroll the scraps. Sprinkle each cookie with sugar.

Bake for 12 to 15 minutes or until the edges begin to turn golden brown. Remove from the sheets and cool on racks. Makes 24 cookies.

Crêpes with Sautéed Apples

6 tart apples
2-4 tablespoons sweet butter
2 tablespoons light brown sugar
1 cup flour
2 tablespoons sugar
1/4 teaspoon salt
3 eggs, beaten
1 tablespoon Calvados or applejack
2 cups milk
2 tablespoons butter, melted
melted butter for pan
vanilla ice cream, softened

Pare, core and thinly slice the apples. Melt the 2 tablespoons of the butter in a skillet, add the apple slices.

Sauté uncovered over a high heat until the apple slices become soft and slightly brown. Sprinkle with the light brown sugar. Remove from the heat and keep warm.

In a large bowl sift together the flour, sugar and salt. Add the eggs, Calvados and milk, stir until well combined. Add the melted butter, stir only to blend. Set the batter aside for 20-30 minutes.

Heat the crêpe pan and coat with some of the melted butter. Pour about 2 tablespoons of batter into the pan, coat evenly. Cook over a moderate heat for 2 minutes. Flip the crêpe and cook an additional 30 seconds. Turn onto a plate and repeat the above process until all the batter is used.

Place each crêpe on a plate and fill with some of the apple mixture. Fold over and top with vanilla ice cream. Serves 6.

Crêpes with
Sautéed Apples

Flan

42 | Flan

1/4 cup sugar
1/2 cup sugar
3 eggs
3 cups milk
1/2 teaspoons vanilla extract
Preheat the oven to 350 degrees F.

In a saucepan heat the 1/4 cup sugar until it becomes a light brown syrup. Coat the sides and bottom of a custard dish or medium soufflé dish with the syrup. Set aside to cool.

In a mixing bowl beat the eggs, and the remaining sugar. Add the milk and vanilla extract, beat well.

Pour the mixture into the prepared pan. Set the dish in a pan of hot water and bake for 30 minutes or until a knife inserted into the center comes out clean. Serves 4.

Tart Dough

1 cup flour
1 1/2 tablespoons sugar
1/4 teaspoon salt
6 tablespoons sweet butter, softened
1 egg yolk
1/2 teaspoon vanilla extract
1 tablespoon ice water

In a large bowl combine the flour, sugar and salt. Cut in the butter with two knives or a pastry blender. When the mixture is well blended, add the egg, vanilla extract and ice water. Combine with your fingers until the dough forms a ball. Transfer the dough to plastic wrap and chill for 30 minutes.

When ready to use, roll the dough out on a lightly floured surface and transfer to the tart pan. Fit into the pan and prick the surface with a fork. Place aluminum foil on top of the dough and weight with beans, rice or pie weights. Bake in a 400 degrees F. oven for 10 minutes or until lightly brown. Use according to recipe.

Lemon Tart

1 tablespoon unflavored gelatin
1/2 cup fresh lemon juice
6 egg yolks
3/4 cup sugar
freshly grated rind of 1-2 lemons
6 egg whites
1 9-inch tart pastry

Preheat oven to 400 degrees F.

Fit the pastry into a 9-inch tart pan and bake with beans or weights as directed in basic recipe. After removing aluminum foil bake for 5 minutes longer, or until golden.

In a small bowl, soften the gelatin in the lemon juice.

In a medium size bowl, beat the egg yolks and sugar until thick and light, about 3 to 4 minutes. Add the lemon rind and stir. Transfer this mixture to a saucepan.

Cook, stirring constantly, over a medium heat until the mixture is very thick, approximately 5 to 8 minutes. Remove from the heat and stir in the gelatin and lemon juice mixture. Continue stirring until thoroughly combined. Turn the mixture into a large bowl and cool.

In a separate bowl beat the egg whites until firm, but not dry. Carefully fold the egg whites into the lemon mixture.

Transfer the mixture to the tart pan. If there is too much filling do not use it all. Smooth the top. Place in the oven and bake only until the top browns slightly, approximately 5 minutes. Remove from the oven and cool before serving. Serves 6.

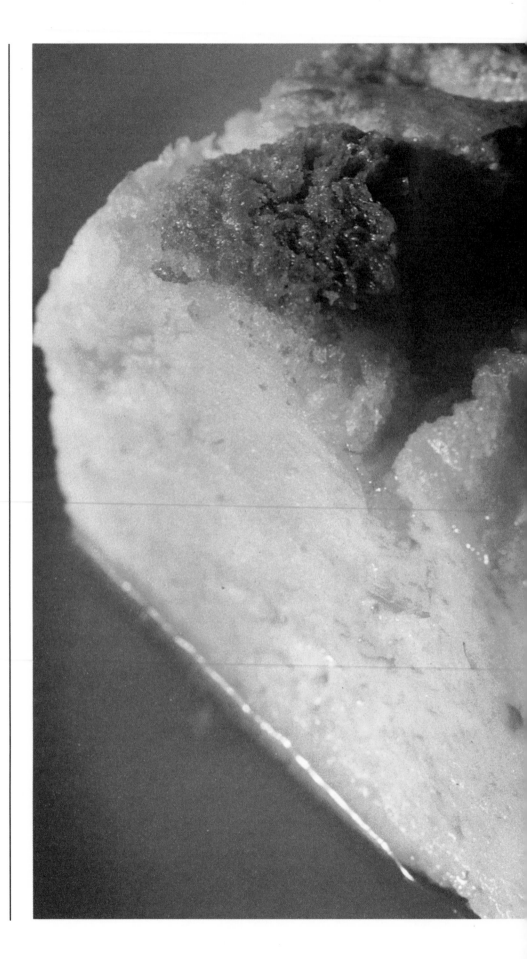

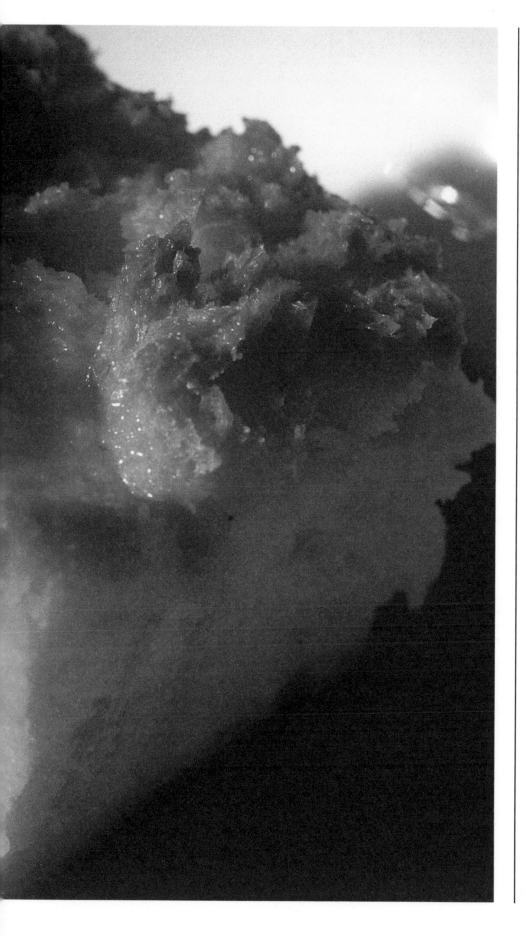

Bread Pudding

46 Bread Pudding

1 cup raisins
1/2 cup Madeira or sherry
10 to 12 slices of stale white bread, crusts removed
butter
4 large eggs
1/3 cup plus 1 tablespoon sugar
1/8 teaspoon salt
2 cups milk
2 cups half and half
heavy cream for whipping

Place the raisins in a small bowl and cover with the Madeira. Allow to sit for 30 minutes. Drain and set aside. Reserve the liquid for flavoring the heavy cream.

Butter the bread slices on one side only.

Generously butter a 2-quart baking dish. Place the slices of bread, buttered side down in the dish. Between each layer sprinkle the raisins.

Beat the eggs lightly in a mixing bowl. Add the sugar, salt, milk and half and half. Transfer this mixture to a saucepan and heat briefly. Using a fine strainer, pour the mixture through the strainer over the bread slices. Allow the mixture to stand for 30 minutes.

Preheat the oven to 325 degrees F.

Cover the baking dish or place a place of aluminum foil over it. Place the dish in a larger pan and add enough hot water to come half way up the sides of the baking dish. Place in the oven and bake for 30 minutes. Remove and cover and bake 30 minutes longer, or until the top of the pudding is a golden brown. Remove from the oven and cool to room temperature, chill if desired.

When ready to serve, whip the heavy cream using the reserved liquid for flavoring. Serves 6.

Pecan Pie

3 eggs
1/4 teaspoon salt
3/4 cup sugar
1/2 cup melted butter
1 cup dark corn syrup
1 1/2 cups pecan halves
1 8 or 9-inch pie pastry

Preheat the oven to 450 degrees F.

Line the pie pan with the pastry and prick all over with a fork. Cover with aluminum foil and weight with beans, rice or pie weights. Bake for 5 to 7 minutes. Remove the pie shell. Reduce the heat to 425 degrees F.

In a medium size bowl beat the eggs and salt. Beat in the sugar. Fold in the butter and the corn syrup, mix well.

Turn the mixture into the pie shell. Sprinkle the pecans over the pie surface and bake for 10 minutes. Reduce the heat to 325 degrees F. and bake for 30 minutes longer. Remove from the oven and allow to cool. Serves 6.

48

Pecan Pie

Apple-Raisin-Nut Tart

50 | Apple-Raisin-Nut Tart

1 sheet frozen puff pastry, thawed
3 Granny Smith apples, peeled, cored and thinly sliced
1/4 cup dark raisins
1/4 cup white raisins
1/2 cup pecans, chopped
2 tablespoons sweet butter, melted
2 tablespoons sugar
1/4 cup apricot jam
1 teaspoon honey or 1 teaspoon light corn syrup

Preheat the oven to 400 degrees F.

Place the pastry into a 9-inch tart pan, prick the surface with a fork.

Sprinkle the pastry with the raisins and nuts. Place the apple slices over the raisin-nut mixture, in an overlapping circular pattern. Brush the butter over the apple slices and sprinkle with the sugar. Bake in the oven for 30-40 minutes or until the apples are tender and the pastry is nicely browned.

In a saucepan combine the jam and honey or corn syrup. Heat until warm, approximately 2 minutes. Brush over the tart. Serves 6.

Apricot Tart

1 9-inch tart pastry
1 10-ounce jar apricot preserves
2 tablespoons rum
1 large can apricot halves, drained
whipped cream

Preheat oven to 425 degrees F.

Fit the pastry into a tart pan and prick all over. Line with aluminum foil, weight with beans or pie weights. Bake for 15 minutes or until the bottom is set. Remove the foil and weights and bake for an additional 3 minutes. Cool on rack.

Place the apricot preserves in a saucepan and heat until they begin to boil. Lower the heat and simmer, stirring constantly, for 2 minutes or until thin. Add the rum and cool.

Brush the apricot-rum mixture over the bottom of the tart pan. Place the apricot halves in the bottom of the pan, cut side down. Brush the remaining apricot glaze over the fruit. Serve with whipped cream if desired. Serves 6.

Carrot Cake

2 cups flour
1 1/3 cups sugar
1 teaspoon cinnamon
1 teaspoon ground nutmeg
1 teaspoon baking soda
1/2 teaspoon salt
3/4 cup buttermilk
3 eggs, beaten lightly
1/2 cup vegetable oil
2 teaspoons vanilla extract
2 cups finely grated peeled carrots
3/4 cup crushed can pineapple, drained
1 cup chopped pecans

FROSTING
3/4 cup confectioners' sugar
3 ounces cream cheese, softened
1 1/2 tablespoons milk
1 teaspoon vanilla extract

Preheat the oven to 350 degrees F. Butter a 9 x 13-inch oblong pan.

In a medium size bowl combine the flour, sugar, cinnamon, nutmeg, baking soda and salt.

In a large bowl, combine the buttermilk, eggs, oil and vanilla. Add the flour mixture and stir until well blended. Add the carrots, pineapple and pecan, stir well.

Pour into the prepared dish and bake for 45 minutes or until a cake tester inserted into the center of the cake comes out clean. Transfer cake to rack and cool. When cool frost with cream cheese frosting, as follows:

Sift the confectioners' sugar into a small bowl. Set aside.

In a medium bowl, combine the cream cheese and milk and beat until soft and well blended. Gradually beat in the sugar. Add the vanilla extract and blend. Use immediately. Serves 6.

Carrot Cake

Chocolate Cream Pie

54 | Chocolate Cream Pie

3/4 cup sugar
1/2 cup flour
1/4 teaspoon salt
1 cup milk
1 cup half and half
2 ounces unsweetened chocolate
3 egg yolks
2 tablespoons butter
1 teaspoon vanilla extract
1/2 teaspoon almond extract
1 9-inch baked pie crust
heavy cream for whipping

In the top of a double boiler combine the sugar, flour and salt.
Add the milk and half and half to this mixture and stir. Add the
unsweetened chocolate. Cook over hot but not boiling water until
the mixture thickens, approximately 8-10 minutes. Remove from
the heat.

   Place the egg yolks in a medium size bowl and beat lightly.
Stirring constantly, pour some of the hot mixture into the eggs.
Be careful not to curdle the yolks. Stir until smooth and then add
the eggs to the hot milk mixture. Return to the heat, and cook
until thickened. Remove from the heat and add the butter, vanilla
extract and almond extract. Mix well.

   Turn the mixture into the baked pie shell and top with whipped
cream if desired. Refrigerate until ready to serve. Serves 8.

Chocolate Pudding

1 cup milk
1 cup light cream or half and half
1 1/2 tablespoons sugar
1 1/2 cups semisweet chocolate pieces
6 egg yolks
1/2 teaspoon almond extract

In the top of a double boiler, combine the milk, light cream and sugar. Over boiling water, heat the mixture until it is almost at the boiling point, but has not boiled.

Remove from the heat and add the chocolate. Stir until all the pieces are completely dissolved.

In a small bowl beat the egg yolks. Gradually, beat the yolks into the hot chocolate mixture. Return the top of the double boiler back to the heat and cook over boiling water for 3-5 minutes, or until the mixture is very thick.

Remove from the heat and add the almond extract. Pour the pudding into 6 Pyrex dishes, ramekins or custard cups. Cool to room temperature and then refrigerate. Serves 6.

Lime-Mint-Vodka Sorbet

1 cup orange juice
1 cup water
3 tablespoons fresh mint, chopped
3 tablespoons sugar
1 tablespoon lemon juice
1 egg white
1/3 cup vodka

Put the orange juice, water, mint, sugar and lemon juice in a food processor or blender. Process until the mint leaves are tiny little flecks.

Pour into a freezer ice cube tray. Freeze until almost solid. Remove the cubes and put into a food processor or blender. Add the egg white and vodka. Process until the cubes have become a thick slush.

Pour the sorbet into a bowl and return the mixture to the freezer. Freeze until the desired texture is obtained. Serves 6.

56

Lime-Mint-Vodka
Sorbet

Apricot Sorbet

58 | Apricot Sorbet

2 cups apricots, halved and pitted
3 tablespoons sugar
1/8 teaspoon allspice
1/2 cup water
1 tablespoon lemon juice
1 egg white

Combine all the ingredients except the egg white in a food processor or blender. Process until the apricots have fully mixed with the lemon juice.

Pour into a ice cube tray. Freeze. Remove the cubes from the tray and put into a food processor or blender. Add the egg white and process until the mixture becomes slushy.

Pour the sorbet into a bowl and return the mixture to the freezer. The sorbet is ready when the mixture has frozen to a firm texture. Serves 6.

Raspberry Sorbet

1 1/2 cups white wine
1 cup raspberries, washed
2 tablespoons sugar
1/4 cup water
1 tablespoon brandy

Combine the wine and raspberries in a food processor or blender. Process until the raspberries are minced. Add the sugar, water and brandy. Process again and pour the liquid into an ice cube tray.

Freeze until the cubes are almost hard. Remove the cubes and put into a food processor or blender. Blend until the mixture is thick.

Pour the sorbet into a bowl and return the mixture to the freezer. Freeze until the desired texture, soft or firm, is obtained. Serves 6.

Strawberry Tart

1 9-inch tart pastry
2 cups cleaned, hulled and sliced fresh strawberries
1/3 cup sugar
1 1/2 tablespoons quick-cooking tapioca
1 jar apricot jam
2 tablespoons orange flavored liqueur
heavy cream for whipping

Preheat the oven to 425 degrees F.

Combine the strawberries and sugar in a bowl, set aside until the strawberries have given off 1 cup of liquid.

Fit the pastry into the tart pan. Prick the bottom of the pan with a fork and line with aluminum foil. Weight the foil with beans, rice or pie weights. Bake for 10 to 15 minutes or until the bottom is set and the edges are brown. ·

Remove from the oven and continue to bake for another 3 minutes without the foil and weights. Set aside on a rack to cool.

In a saucepan mix 1 cup of the strawberry liquid with the tapioca. Heat until the tapioca is dissolved. Remove from the heat and cool for 15 minutes. Add to the strawberries and mix well.

In a small saucepan heat the apricot jam, stir constantly, until the jam comes to a boil. Reduce the heat and continue to cook until the jam gets thinner, about 2 minutes. Add the orange liqueur to the jam and cool.

Brush the bottom of the tart shell with apricot glaze and spoon the strawberries into the shell. Smooth the top and use the remaining glaze to brush the top of the tart. Accompany with lightly beaten cream if desired. Serves 6.

VARIATION
Place pastry into 4 individual tart pans and proceed with the remainder of the recipe as above.

Raspberry Sorbet

Fruit Salad with
Peanut Dressing

62 | Fruit Salad with Peanut Dressing

2 bananas, peeled and sliced 1/4-inch thick
1 mango, peeled, seeded and cut into 1/2-inch chunks
1 grapefruit, peeled and cut into sections
2 oranges, peeled and cut into sections
1/2 cup smooth peanut butter
1/2 cup vegetable oil
1/4 cup granulated sugar
juice of 2 lemons
1/2 teaspoon powdered ginger
1/2 teaspoon black pepper
1 tablespoon dark rum
1/2 cup chopped peanuts

Mix all the fruits together in a serving bowl and chill for 1 hour.

Mix all the remaining ingredients, except the chopped peanuts, in a shaker jar or blender until smooth and syrupy in consistency. Let stand 1 hour for flavors to blend. Serve salad with dressing poured over and chopped peanuts sprinkled on top. Serves 6.

Chocolate Ice Cream

2 ounces unsweetened chocolate
2 cups milk
3/4 cup sugar
a pinch of salt
1 teaspoon vanilla extract
1/2 teaspoon almond extract
2 cups heavy cream

In the top of a double boiler, over hot, not boiling water, melt the chocolate in the milk. Add the sugar and salt. Remove from the heat. Beat the mixture with a whisk or electric hand mixer until it is cool. When cool add the vanilla extract, almond extract and cream. Transfer to ice cream machine and process according to manufacturer's directions. Serves 8.

Strawberry-Banana Ice Cream

2 cups hulled strawberries
2 cups sliced bananas
3/4 cup sugar
2 cups heavy cream
2 cups light cream

Place the strawberries and bananas in a food processor along with the sugar. Process for 15 seconds or until the mixture is thick but not liquid.

Pour into a bowl and combine with the heavy cream and light cream. Transfer to ice cream machine and process according to manufacturer's directions. Serves 10.

Maple-Walnut Ice Cream

1 1/2 cups milk
3/4 cup sugar
a pinch of salt
3 egg yolks, beaten
1 tablespoon pure maple extract
2 cups heavy cream
1 cup toasted chopped walnuts

In a saucepan over a low heat, scald the milk but do not bring it to a boil. Add the sugar and salt and stir to dissolve. Remove from the heat.

Add the milk very slowly to the beaten egg yolks. Beat until well blended. Transfer to the top of a double boiler and cook over boiling water until the mixture is very thick. Remove from the heat and chill.

When custard is cold stir in the maple extract, heavy cream and chopped walnuts. Transfer to ice cream machine and process according to manufacturer's directions. Serves 10.

Maple-Walnut
Ice Cream

66 | Biscotti

3 1/2 cups flour
1 tablespoon baking powder
1/2 cup low-fat margarine, softened
3/4 cup sugar
5 eggs
2 tablespoons freshly grated lemon peel
1 cup pine nuts
3/4 cup shelled pistachio nuts
1 egg white, lightly beaten
sugar for sprinkling

In a large bowl, or on a sheet of waxed paper, combine the flour and baking powder.

In a large bowl combine the margarine and sugar and beat until fluffy and light in color. Add the eggs, lemon peel and vanilla and beat until the mixture is smooth and thick.

Add the flour gradually and mix well after each addition. Add the nuts and stir.

Gather the dough into a ball and divide it into 3 equal parts. Wrap each in plastic wrap and refrigerate for 5 hours or until easy to handle.

Preheat the oven to 350 degrees F. Spray two baking sheets with low-calorie cooking spray.

Remove the dough from the refrigerator and transfer each section to a lightly-floured surface. Shape each portion into a large log. Place 2 of the logs on 1 sheet about 4-5 inches apart, place the remaining log on the other sheet. Brush each log with the egg white and sprinkle with the sugar.

Bake for 30-35 minutes or until the dough has flattened some-what and the top is slightly cracked.

Remove the sheets from the oven. Using a large metal spatula, loosen the dough from the sheet and allow it to cool for 8 to 10 minutes. Carefully transfer the logs, one at a time, to a cutting board.

With a large knife, slice each log into diagonal slices. Return to the baking sheets only after they have been wiped clean. The slices can be placed close together. Bake for 10-15 minutes, turning twice, until the biscotti are dry and lightly toasted. Remove from oven and cool on racks. Makes approximately 40 biscotti.

Oatmeal-Raisin Cookies

1 egg beaten
1/2 cup sugar
1/2 cup low-fat margarine, melted
2 teaspoons molasses
2 teaspoons low-fat milk
1 cup quick-cooking rolled oats (not instant)
1/2 cup raisins
3/4 cup flour
1/2 teaspoon cinnamon
1/4 teaspoon baking soda
1/4 teaspoon salt

Preheat the oven to 325 degree F. Lightly grease two baking sheets. Set aside.

In a large mixing bowl combine the egg, sugar, melted margarine, molasses and milk. Mix well.

In another bowl, combine the oats, flour, cinnamon, baking soda and salt. Stir in the raisins. Add to the first mixture and combine until well-blended.

Drop the dough by heaping teaspoons about 2 inches apart on the greased baking sheets. Bake for 10 to 12 minutes or until cookies are browned. Cool cookies on rack. Makes approximately 36 cookies.

Oatmeal-Raisin
Cookies

Sugar Cookies

70 | Sugar Cookies

3 egg whites, at room temperature
2/3 cup vegetable oil
2 teaspoons pure vanilla extract
1 teaspoon freshly grated lemon rind or orange rind
3/4 cup sugar
2 cups flour
1/2 teaspoon salt
2 teaspoons baking powder

Preheat the oven to 400 degrees F.

In a large bowl, beat the egg whites with a fork. Add the oil, vanilla and lemon or orange rind and stir. Add the sugar and continue stirring until the mixture beings to thicken.

Onto a large sheet of waxed paper sift the flour, salt and baking powder. Add this to the first mixture and stir until well blended.

Drop dough by heaping teaspoons onto ungreased cookie sheets, spacing them about 2 inches apart. Dip the bottom of a glass in oil and then in sugar. Flatten each mound of dough with the bottom of the glass. Repeat the oil and sugar process as needed. Bake in the oven for 8-10 minutes or until lightly browned. Remove from the oven and transfer to cooling racks. Makes approximately 48 cookies.

Almond Wafers

4 egg whites
1/8 teaspoon salt
4 tablespoons flour
6 tablespoons low-fat margarine, melted
1/2 teaspoon pure almond extract
1 teaspoon pure vanilla extract
1 cup coarsely chopped blanched almonds

Preheat the oven to 325 degrees F. Heavily grease two baking sheets with low-fat margarine or low-calorie cooking spray.

In the large bowl of an electric mixer, beat the egg whites with the salt until foamy. Add the sugar, 1 tablespoon at a time, beating constantly until the mixture is stiff and shiny.

Sift the flour over the egg white mixture. Fold gently. Combine the margarine, almond extract, vanilla extract and almonds. Add this to the egg white mixture and fold thoroughly but gently.

Drop the batter by teaspoonfuls, spaced 3 inches apart, onto the baking sheets. Flatten with fingers into a 2 1/2 -inch circle.

Bake for 10 minutes. Remove from the oven. Using a wide spatula remove one cookie at a time and curve each around a rolling pin. Allow cookie to stay on the pin until it has cooled. Remove when cool and store in airtight containers. Makes approximately 30 cookies.

Almond Meringues

3/4 cup blanched almonds
1/4 cup amaretto or almond-flavored liqueur
2 large egg whites, at room temperature
1/2 cream of tartar
1/2 cup sugar
1/2 teaspoon pure almond extract
1/4 cup blanched, ground almonds

In a small bowl combine the ground, blanched almonds and the liqueur. Set aside. Place the egg whites in the medium-sized bowl of an electric mixture. Beat until foamy. Add the cream of tartar and continue beating the egg whites until they hold a soft peak.

Gradually add the sugar and the almond extract. Continue beating until the mixture becomes stiff and holds a stiff peak. Carefully fold in the ground almond mixture.

Preheat the oven to 325 degrees F. Prepare baking sheets by covering them with parchment or waxed paper. If necessary, attach the paper to the sheet by putting a drop of meringue mixture on the underside of each corner. Drop the batter by teaspoonsful, 2 inches apart on the sheets. Smooth the tops of the cookies and press a sliced almond into the center of each cookie.

Bake for 15-20 minutes or until the meringues are dry to the touch. If the cookies begin to brown, reduce the oven temperature to 300 degrees F. and open the oven door slightly.

Remove from the oven. Let cookies cool on the sheets for 3 minutes before transferring them to wire racks. Cool completely before storing in airtight containers. Makes approximately 24 cookies.

Almond Meringues

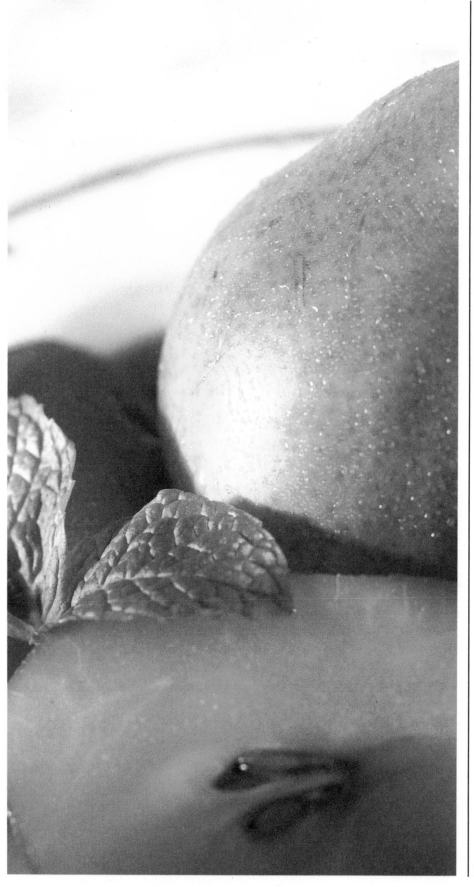

Pears in Red Wine

74 | Spiced Stuffed Figs in Port

1/2 cup chopped nuts (almonds or pecans are best)
3 tablespoons low-fat margarine
2 tablespoons brown sugar
1 pound dried figs
1 cup ruby port

In a bowl, cream together the nuts, margarine and brown sugar.

Make a small incision in each fig and stuff with a teaspoonful of the nut mixture.

Place the figs in a baking dish and pour over the port. Cover the dish with foil and bake in a 350 degree F. oven for about 20 minutes. Let cool.

Arrange the figs on individual serving plates and pour some of the port over each. Serves 6.

Pears in Red Wine

6 ripe Bartlett pears
1 cup red wine
1 cup sugar

Peel the pears, leave stems. Combine the wine and sugar in a saucepan, bring the mixture to a boil and stir until the sugar is dissolved, boil over a low heat for 8 minutes.

Add the pears, cover and poach over a low heat for 20 minutes or until tender. Serve with poaching syrup. Serves 6.

Thumbprint Cookies

1 cup sweet butter, softened
1 cup sugar
2 teaspoons pure vanilla extract
2 eggs, separated
2 1/2 cups flour, sifted
1 cup finely chopped pecans
raspberry or blackberry jam

In a medium-size bowl beat the butter, sugar, vanilla, and egg yolks at a high speed until light and fluffy. Gradually stir in the flour with a wooden spoon. Gather the dough in a ball and wrap in plastic. Refrigerate 4 hours or until firm.

Preheat the oven to 300 degrees F.

Form the dough into balls by using a level teaspoon. Dip the balls into the egg whites and then roll them in the chopped pecans.

Arrange the balls on ungreased baking sheets, approximately 1 inch apart. Using your thumb or the end of a wooden spoon, make an indentation in each cookie. Fill the indentation with the jam.

Bake cookies for 20 minutes or until golden. Remove to cooling racks. Makes approximately 48 cookies.

Snickerdoodles

1 cup sweet butter, softened
1 1/2 cups plus 2 tablespoons sugar
2 eggs
2 3/4 cups flour
2 teaspoons cream of tartar
1 teaspoon baking soda
1/4 teaspoon salt
2 teaspoons cinnamon

In a large bowl beat the butter until soft, add 1 1/2 cups of the sugar and the eggs and continue beating until light and fluffy.

In another bowl combine the flour, cream of tartar, baking soda and salt. Add this to the first mixture and stir until well blended. Cover the bowl and refrigerate for 1 hour.

Preheat the oven to 375 degrees F. In a small bowl combine the remaining sugar and cinnamon. Shape the dough into balls approximately 2 inches in diameter and roll in the cinnamon sugar. Place the balls 3 inches apart on ungreased baking sheets.

Bake the cookies for 12-15 minutes or until golden. Remove to cooling racks when done. Makes approximately 24 large cookies. (Make sure to leave plenty of room between the cookies on the sheet, these cookies will puff up and then flatten out as they bake.)

Snickerdoodles

Rolled Spice Cookies

78 | Peanut Butter Kisses

2 cups smooth peanut butter
1 1/4 cups sugar
2 eggs
48 milk chocolate kisses

Preheat the oven to 350 degrees F. In a medium-size bowl combine the peanut butter, sugar and eggs until well blended.

With well-floured hands (the dough will be sticky) form level tablespoons of the dough and roll it into balls. Place balls approximately 2 inches apart on ungreased baking sheets.

Bake the cookies for 12-15 minutes or until the tops begin to crack and the cookies are dry to the touch. Remove the sheets from the oven and immediately press a chocolate kiss into the center of each cookie. Allow the cookies to cool on the sheets for 2 minutes before removing to racks to cool. Makes approximately 48 cookies.

Rolled Spice Cookies

4 cups flour
1 teaspoon ground cinnamon
1 teaspoon ground nutmeg
1/2 teaspoon ground ginger
1/4 teaspoon ground cloves
1/2 teaspoon salt
1 1/2 cups sweet butter, softened
1 cup sugar
1 egg
1 teaspoon pure vanilla extract

ICING
1 cup sifted confectioners sugar
1/4 teaspoon salt
1/2 teaspoon vanilla extract
1 1/2 tablespoons heavy cream
 red or green food coloring

In a large bowl combine the flour, cinnamon, nutmeg, ginger, cloves and salt.In another large bowl beat the butter and sugar together until light and fluffy. Add the egg and the vanilla extract, beat until blended. With the mixer on the lowest speed, gradually add the flour-spice mixture. Continue mixing until blended.

Separate the dough into 3 equal pieces, flatten each piece and wrap in plastic wrap. Refrigerate until firm, about 1 hour.

Preheat the oven to 375 degrees F. Remove dough from the refrigerator. On a lightly floured surface, roll the dough, one piece at a time, to 1/4-inch thickness. Using floured cookie cutters, cut into desired shapes.

Place the cookies 1 inch apart on ungreased baking sheets and bake for 10-12 minutes or until the edges are just brown. Transfer cookies to racks to cool. Continue re-rolling the scraps until all the dough has been used. After cookies are cool decorate with icing, as follows: In a small bowl combine the sugar, salt and vanilla extract. Add the cream and stir until blended. Add desired food coloring, stir to blend. Apply to cooled cookies with a spatula or pastry tube. Allow the icing to dry. Makes approximately 48 cookies.

Sugary Lemon Cut-Outs

1 cup sweet butter, softened
3/4 cup sugar
1/2 teaspoon salt
1 egg
1 egg yolk
2 tablespoons fresh lemon juice
1 teaspoon pure vanilla or almond extract
4 cups flour
white, red and green sugar for decorating

Combine the butter, 3/4 cup sugar and salt together in a large bowl, beat until light and fluffy. Add the egg, the egg yolk, lemon juice and vanilla extract, beat until blended. With the mixer on the lowest speed, gradually add the flour, beat until just mixed.

Form the dough into a large ball, then separate into 2 equal pieces. Wrap each half in plastic and refrigerate for 4 hours or until firm.

Preheat the oven to 350 degrees F. Grease baking sheets with butter. Remove the dough from the refrigerator. On a lightly floured surface, roll the dough, one piece at a time, to approximately 1/8-inch thickness. Cut with desired Christmas cookie cutters. Place each cookie on the sheets, approximately 1 inch apart. Sprinkle cookies with white, red or green sugar.

Bake for 10-12 minutes or until the edges are just light brown. Remove from the oven and transfer cookies to racks to cool. Makes approximately 68 cookies.

Sugary Lemon
Cut-Outs

Wedding Cakes

Wedding Cakes

1 cup sweet butter, softened
1/2 cup confectioners' sugar
1 teaspoon pure vanilla extract
1/4 teaspoon salt
2 cups flour
confectioners' sugar

In a large bowl, cream the butter until light and fluffy.
Add the sugar, vanilla extract and salt. Beat until well blended.
Add the flour and stir until well mixed. Cover the bowl and refrigerate for 30 minutes or until dough is firm enough to handle.

Preheat the oven to 375 degrees F.

Remove the dough from the refrigerator and shape into 1-inch balls. Space 1 inch apart on ungreased baking sheets. Bake for 12-15 minutes or until light golden in color.

Remove from the oven and transfer cookies to cooling racks. Place the cookies close together. While cookies are still warm, dust heavily with confectioners' sugar. Cool completely. Makes approximately 48 cookies.

Lemon-Nut Biscotti

3 1/2 cups flour
1 tablespoon baking powder
1/2 cup low-fat margarine, softened
3/4 cup sugar
5 eggs
2 tablespoons freshly grated lemon peel
1 cup pine nuts
3/4 cup shelled pistachio nuts
1 egg white, lightly beaten
sugar for sprinkling

In a large bowl, or on a sheet of waxed paper, combine the flour and baking powder.

In a large bowl combine the margarine and sugar and beat until fluffy and light in color. Add the eggs, lemon peel and vanilla and beat until the mixture is smooth and thick.

Add the flour gradually and mix well after each addition. Add the nuts and stir.

Gather the dough into a ball and divide it into 3 equal parts. Wrap each part in plastic wrap and refrigerate for 5 hours or until easy to handle.

Preheat the oven to 350 degrees F. Spray baking sheets with a low-calorie cooking spray.

Remove the dough from the refrigerator and transfer each section to a lightly floured surface. Shape each portion into a large log. Place 2 of the logs on 1 sheet about 4-5 inches apart, place the remaining log on the other sheet. Brush each log with the egg white and sprinkle with the sugar.

Bake for 30 to 35 minutes or until the dough has flattened somewhat and the top is slightly cracked.

Remove the sheets from the oven. Using a large metal spatula, loosen the dough from the sheet and allow it to cool for 8 to 10 minutes. Carefully transfer the logs, one at a time, to a cutting board.

With a large knife, slice each log into diagonal slices. Return to the baking sheets only after they have been wiped clean. The slices may be placed close together. Bake for 10-15 minutes, turning twice, until the biscotti are dry and lightly toasted. Remove from oven and cool on racks. Makes approximately 40 biscotti.

Crescents

Crescents

1 cup sweet butter, softened
1/2 cup confectioners sugar
2 teaspoons pure vanilla extract
1/4 teaspoon salt
1 3/4 cups flour
1 cup finely ground walnuts
1/2 cup sugar

In a large bowl cream together the butter, confectioners sugar, vanilla extract and salt until light and fluffy. Add the flour and walnuts and stir until well blended. Cover the bowl and chill until the dough is firm enough to handle, approximately 45 minutes.

Preheat the oven to 300 degrees F.

Remove the dough from the refrigerator. Working on a lightly floured board, break off small pieces of dough and roll into finger-thick strips. Cut the strips into 2-inch lengths. Taper the ends and shape into crescents.

Place the cookies 1 inch apart on ungreased baking sheets. Bake for 18-20 minutes or until cookies are firm.

Remove from the oven. While the cookies are still warm roll them in the sugar. Be careful not to remove them from the sheets too quickly or they may crumble. Cool on wire racks. Makes approximately 60 cookies.

Hermits

1/2 cup sugar
1/3 cup sweet butter, softened
1 egg
3 cups flour
1/2 teaspoon salt
1 teaspoon cinnamon
1/2 teaspoon grated nutmeg
1/2 cup molasses
1/2 cup buttermilk
1 cup raisins

Preheat the oven to 350 degrees F. Grease baking sheets with butter and set aside.

In a mixing bowl cream together the sugar and butter until light and fluffy. Beat in the egg.

Combine the flour, salt, cinnamon and nutmeg together in a bowl. In a measuring cup, combine the molasses with the buttermilk. Add the molasses mixture alternately with the flour to the creamed sugar and butter. Stir in the raisins.

Drop the dough by teaspoonfuls approximately 1 inch apart on the baking sheets. Bake for 8-10 minutes or until lightly browned. Cool on wire rack. Makes approximately 72 cookies.

Frosted Lemon Butter Balls

1 cup sweet butter, softened
1/2 cup confectioners sugar
1 1/2 cups flour
3/4 cup cornstarch
1/4 teaspoon salt
2 teaspoons grated lemon rind
1 cup finely chopped blanched almonds

FROSTING
1 cup confectioners' sugar
2 tablespoons sweet butter, melted
1 tablespoon lemon juice

Preheat the oven to 350 degrees F. Lightly grease baking sheets and set aside.

In a large bowl, cream together the butter and sugar until light and fluffy.

Sift the flour, cornstarch and salt together onto a piece of waxed paper. Add to the butter mixture, mix well. Add the lemon rind and stir.

Shape the dough into 1-inch balls and roll in the chopped almonds. Press nuts in gently. Place cookies 1 inch apart on baking sheets. Bake for 15 minutes. Remove from the oven and transfer to wire racks to cool.

To make the frosting, in a small bowl combine the confectioners' sugar, melted butter and lemon juice. Stir until smooth. Drizzle frosting over cooled cookies. Allow frosting to harden before storing cookies. Makes approximately 40 cookies.

Frosted Lemon
Butter Balls

Raspberry Crumb Bars

Hazelnut Butter Balls

1/2 cup sweet butter, softened
1/4 cup sugar
1 egg, separated
1 tablespoon white rum
1/2 teaspoon pure vanilla extract
1 cup flour
1/2 cup finely chopped hazelnuts

In a medium-size bowl, cream together the butter and sugar until light and fluffy. Add the egg yolk, white rum and vanilla extract. Beat until well blended. Add the flour and mix well. Cover the bowl and refrigerate 4 hours or overnight.

Preheat oven to 325 degrees F. Lightly grease baking sheets.

Remove the dough from the refrigerator. Form the dough into 3/4-inch balls. Place the chopped hazelnuts in one bowl, and the egg white in another bowl. Lightly beat the egg white.

Dip the top of each ball into the egg white and then into the hazelnuts. Place cookies, nut side up, 1 inch apart on a baking sheets. Bake for 12-15 minutes or until golden brown.

Remove from the oven and transfer to racks for cooling. Makes approximately 42 cookies.

Raspberry Crumb Bars

1 3/4 cups flour
1/2 teaspoon baking soda
1 cup sweet butter, softened
1 cup firmly packed light brown sugar
1 1/2 cups quick-cooking rolled oats (not instant)
1 cup raspberry jam

Preheat the oven to 400 degrees F. With butter, grease a 13 x 9 x 2-inch baking pan. Set aside.

In a small bowl, combine the flour and the baking soda. Set aside.

In a medium-size bowl cream together the butter and the brown sugar until fluffy and light in color. Add the flour mixture and stir until well blended. Add the oats and mix well. This may be easiest to do with your hands.

Press half the dough into the prepared pan. Spread the layer evenly with the jam. Crumble the remaining dough over the top. Pat gently.

Bake for 20-25 minutes or until lightly browned. Remove from the oven and cool in the pan on a wire rack. Cut into bars while still warm. Serve warm or cool. Makes approximately 30 bars.

Almond Macaroons

1 1/4 cups slivered blanched almonds
3/4 cup sugar
3 egg whites
1/4 teaspoon ground nutmeg
candied cherries or extra slivered blanched almonds

In a food processor or blender grind the nuts until they are very fine.

In a medium-size saucepan, combine the nuts, sugar and egg whites. Cook over a medium heat, stirring constantly for 10 minutes or until the mixture begins to thicken and holds its shape when pressed with a wooden spoon. Remove from the heat and add the nutmeg.

Drop the mixture by level tablespoons onto baking sheets that have been buttered and lightly floured. Allow the macaroons to stand at room temperature until they have cooled.

Preheat the oven to 300 degrees F. Carefully place halves of the candied cherries or slivers of the almonds on the top of the macaroons. Bake for 20 minutes or until just lightly golden. Remove from the baking sheets immediately with a wide spatula. Makes approximately 24 macaroons.

92 | Pinwheel Cookies

1/2 cup sweet butter, softened
1/4 cup solid vegetable shortening
3/4 cup sugar
2 eggs
2 1/2 cups flour
1 teaspoon baking powder
1 teaspoon salt
2 ounces unsweetened chocolate, melted and cooled

In a large bowl combine the butter, shortening, sugar, eggs and vanilla, beat until well mixed.

In a small bowl, combine the flour, baking powder and salt. Stir into the butter mixture and continue stirring until blended.

Carefully divide the dough in half and remove one half from the bowl and wrap it in plastic. To the half remaining in the bowl, add the melted chocolate and stir to mix. Cover and refrigerate both halves for 2 hours or until firm enough to roll.

On a lightly floured board, roll the vanilla dough into a rectangle approximately 12 x 9 inches. Roll the chocolate dough to the same dimensions, carefully place the chocolate dough on top of the vanilla dough. Roll the layers of dough together, beginning at the wide end; roll up tightly. Cover with plastic wrap and chill overnight.

Preheat oven to 400 degrees F.

Cut the dough into slices that are 1/8 inch thick and place on ungreased baking sheets. Bake for 8-10 minutes or until just lightly brown. Remove to racks and cool. Makes approximately 72 cookies.